**Advance Praise for *Words at Play***

"*Words at Play* is a volume marked by profound tensions—celestial to earthy, other to self, light to heavy, formal to free, certainty to doubt—embraced by a love of nature and man, all within forty pages… a treasury of verse."

—Emerson Gilmore, former President of
The Connecticut Poetry Society

"Showcasing a range of local voices, *Words at Play* offers poems from the comic to the spiritual. Many call on nature's solace, long for peace in the face of aging and loss, or express simple joys like winning at Scrabble or sharing a daily routine with a spouse. There's something here for everyone."

—Laurel S. Peterson, Poet Laureate Emeritus
of Norwalk, Connecticut

"In *Words at Play*, a diverse group of Connecticut writers have produced a variety of entertaining and thought-provoking poems. I highly recommend this anthology to lovers of verse; in its pages, there's a poem to please every discerning reader."

—Alison McBain, award-winning poet

# Words at Play

## Selections from the Wilton Poetry Group

Edited by Ed Ahern

Compilation © 2026 Fairfield Scribes & Wilton, CT Poetry Group. All rights reserved. This book or any portion thereof may not be reproduced without permission of the publisher or poetry group, except in the case of critical reviews and other noncommercial uses permitted by law. For permission requests, write to the publisher at fairfieldscribes@gmail.com.

"Identity" & "Ode to Hitchhiker" © 2026 by Sadiqua Azad
"Maybe" & "Colors" © 2026 by Edward Kabak
"Celestial Spheres" & "The Eighth Gate" © 2026 by D. C. Wilkinson
"Oyster Shucker" © 2026 by Wayne Lysobey
"Magic Moments" & "It's the same old song" © 2026 by Dearta Logu Fusaro
"Boggled" & "crumbling…" © 2026 by Adele Evershed
"Voyage" & "Unscheduled Stop" © 2026 by Francie Grace
"For No Reason" & "Pebble on Stone" © 2026 by Ray Rauth
"The Quaking Aspen" & "Again" © 2026 by Debra Wagner
"Love Song" & "Signals" © 2026 by Marsha Whitman
"Cheap Ass Charlie (Love on the Free Range)" © 2026 by Chrisopher Seep
"Airplane" © 2026 by Marsha Temlock
"Silence" & "An Ode to Mourning Doves" © 2026 by Janet Krauss
"Bag of Almonds" © 2026 by Alicia Gignoux
"Epiphyte Lessons" & "Cinquains of the Day" © 2026 by Pamela Klem
"Fast Water Blues" & "Midsummer Moment" © 2026 by Ed Ahern

Cover image by Eyüp Belen
Cover design by Alison McBain

ISBN-13: 978-1-949122-26-8
Fairfield Scribes & Wilton, CT Poetry Group
Fairfield, CT
United States of America

First printing February 2026.

## Listing of Poets

# Sadiqua Azad

## Identity

I am not a noun, I am a verb

I am not my name
I am not my gender
I am not my beliefs
I am not my culture
I am not my race
I am not my nation

I am my deeds
I am my action
I am a process
I am an undertaking
I am loudly thinking
I am a human being

I am not a noun, I am a verb

## Ode to Hitchhiker

Reflect
Inspect
Introspect

This road to within seems long
Long and winding
And I am hitchhiking
On the road
Where questions pop
As milestones
And milestones pop
As questions
And I trek with anticipation
That I will find
Someone
At the terminus
And ask
How do you do?
Who are you?
Is the answer 42?

# Edward Kabak

## Maybe

Maybe the wind is schizophrenic
The sky is depressed when it's blue
Maybe the clouds are catatonic
When the eye of a storm passes through
Maybe the stars have paranoia
Celestially prancing apace
And maybe the moon is often bipolar
Those times it averts its whole face
Maybe the trees and mountains and valleys
Are demented by flowers and rain
Maybe the oceans rivers and gorges
Disordered are flowing insane
Maybe the earth is confused and deluded
Confined by its gravity too
For even the sun was manic-depressive
Until it fell crazy for you.

## Colors

I never knew when a lady was blue
Underneath her color was green
I never knew there's a radiance thru
Which all the colors are seen
I never knew—
I was blind, had no view
Of two glorious jewels in the sky
I never knew
'Til the light shined on you—
I could see the whole world in your eyes
Because—
You're red when impassioned
Purple when holy
And when you're eternal you're green
You're black when you're mystic
And blue when celestial
And sometimes your color's unseen
In the winter you snow me
In the springtime you grow me
In summer I'm lemon you're lime
In the fall you're a feather
That lies on the heather
Your love is the color of time
And you are each hue that's divine

# D. C. Wilkinson

## Celestial Spheres

I was born infinite times
from pregnant silences,
each instance
a bloodbath full of promise.
Countless cells
sparked life divine,
morphed into translucent eggs--
reflections of celestial spheres.
From Cusco to Thebes,
and Axum to Persepolis,
sanctuaries arose,
within delicate,
membranous walls.
I walked among sages,
built temples,
and forged empires.
Time and again,
I was conqueror
and dust.
How many lifetimes
since I last shed my skin
aged a millennium?
Where did it all begin?
Was it here,
on this drifting speck of dust
or somewhere on Andromeda,
Sagittarius or Triangulum?
The dance of life unfolded,
each vessel a cradle,
each breath a thread
woven through
a boundless cosmic tapestry.

## The Eighth Gate

A golden chariot
brought Morpheus
in a dream
bearing a message.
In one breath,
he whispered
that all walls
between dimensions
had collapsed,
Heaven had trembled,
and the Eighth Gate
had opened
in Jerusalem.
I climbed onto the chariot
and glided to the Gate
to see the Promised One.
Around me,
a rapturous event unfolded—
All spacetimes
began merging into one.
Cries of joy
arose from the crowds
as they beheld
an otherworldly presence
emerging from the Gate.
A crown of galaxies
graced His head.
I stood in awe,
petrified.
And then I heard my voice
beneath His words:
"At last,

you have arrived,
my lord!”
Bewildered,
I gazed into
His eyes
and saw my past lives
huddled in there
in quiet repose.

# Wayne Lysobey

## Oyster Shucker

I got me an oyster knife
I thought I'd be a shucker
I tried it on the first one
It was a really stubborn trucker

I tried it on another
This one made me pucker
The shell it sliced my finger
That lousy bivalve mucker

I stuck one right in the hinge
And gave a mighty twist
The oyster did not budge
Now I was getting pissed

I started getting serious
I gave a satisfying curse
I put some muscle into it
Things went from bad to worse

The oyster knife it did slip
Jamming right into my wrist
I was dying for an oyster
Now I just might get my wish

## Dearta Logu Fusaro

### Magic Moments

When the sun rays shine through the dancing leaves
Of brown barked trees
She walks, and the air cascades
Sweet and soft hues of ponderosa

Whenever she is here alone, she feels company
Old friends fifty feet tall invite her in their bubble
And the charming duet of sparrow and chickadee
Grandiosely serenade the mariposa

And she walks and the air cascades
That sour soil of old leaves and moss
Tomorrow to bitterly be replaced
By synthetic smells of citrus and mimosa

She grin-and-bears the new world order
Comfort replaces spirit, and work, life
The chance of these magic moments
Often demoted to the superficial hike

And it is this path in which we burn the earth alive
Slowly step by step and stone by cement
Dwellings with a bush or two, fighting plastic to survive
Comforting the owner and forbidding a bee of its hive

This is the real magic
The natural becoming unnatural
The unnatural walking to evoke the natural
Magic moments

## It’s the same old song

It’s the same old song
In the morning I hear him singing
Late nights too on the front porch
I hear him singing
The shadow he cast on the sun
Long years between us
But with my mom, he is one
And I hear him singing ...
Across the valley and to the river
I see her stepping in
I always walk to her to hold her tender
Cuz she loves from within
I hear him singing ...
Yea woman of mine
Rise and shine
Shine my day
Be my light
Give me a memory I won’t lament
He chose her everyday
How could he ever love again
I will always miss dreaming my dreams with you
You are mine and hers alright
I should have always loved you
right, yes, you are mine and hers alright
don't be an oak
be bamboo that bounces back
do not snap, resist
homemade petulla
swim deep in bubbling oil
memory blisters

*(petulla = fried dough in Albanian)*

## Adele Evershed

### Boggled

Who was that poet—
the one who wrote about God and bogs?
I love that word—bog—
it sits thick in your mouth,
full of everything
you'd rather not see again.
Starting with that softened 'B',
as your lips brush together
like a kiss to a passing life,
then the holy stretching 'O'—
a black hole to fall into
and finally, the phlegmy 'G',
like a miner boggy with black lung,
belting out *Bread of Heaven*
or some other funeral dirge.
Here, there are cranberry bogs—
full of bitterness,
berries only good in pie—
and still—you need a bog full of custard
to stop them tasting like a sacrifice.
I prefer my bogs like my Gods—unknowable,
and as dark as a pint of the black stuff—
foggy-headed, dripping with damp,
where swirling ghosts of bog bodies
dance and are then discarded
like yesterday's news or a virgin martyr.
Do you know there's such a thing as bog butter—
deliberately buried to preserve it in the cool,
still edible centuries later?
I find it strange that I know this—
but can't remember that poet's name.

## crumbling...

I bought peaches
at a farmer's market
nestled in green cardboard
like eggs of some make-believe bird—
the sign offered a quart for five dollars
which seemed an old way
to measure fruit
I squeezed one
checking for ripeness
and it gave softly
promising juice
and long (past) summer nights

The farmer—
who didn't look like she worked the land
wrapped them in white plastic
which felt like a small betrayal

When I got home
only one was ready for eating
the others hiding
under that one perfect peach
were as hard as old snow
and only good for cooking
As I chopped, peeled, and crumbled
the leaves browned
the cicadas dirged
as if they had learned—
sweetness like summer is fleeing
You see—even the sun grows tired
as autumn bends her back
until she is claimed by winter

and all I can do
is wash my hands in the cold sunlight
watch them soften and spot—
another betrayal
but one that's not so small

# Francie Grace

## Voyage

I flew through
the solar system
to get to you

Through frozen wastelands
millions of years old
Terrifying beauty

powerful rivers of ice
silently waiting
to be born

## Unscheduled Stop

Inside the tin can
sardines peruse the news
sweat silently
and think of sweethearts

Lurching forward into the night
the train slows and I open an eye
I don't know why

Beyond the doors
not a single light
The conductor turns the key
ready to lock the fish back in

It's not my stop
but out I pop

## Ray Rauth

### For No Reason

Twenty years ago
I bought my wife a ring,
rubies and diamonds alternating
in a circle of gold.

"I love it," she said, and hugged me.
It fit right, loose enough to slip off,
but not too loose to lose.
She wears it snug against her wedding band.

At night she stores it on her bedside table
in a ceramic box, a little coffin,
big enough for two rings

Soon after this gift she said,
"Never buy me jewelry."

Mysterious, women are jungle cats,
smooth and sleek
they hide at night and preen in the light,
the universe or nothing in their eyes.

## Pebble on Stone

Murmur in the graveyard, the relatives
Pluck a pebble, place it on a stone.
The pebble is a notice: Someone came.
Someone remembered.

Relatives, or strangers.
I cannot find my father's grave;
Roaming wherever I place pebbles on stone—
Iceland, Venice, Danbury, Rome, Seattle—

It's phony anyway. The mind
Is gone, bones soon discard their flesh,
And calcium leaches long before
The pebbles fall.

But fluid as an oily sea, plates
Of crustal Earth will descend into the depths,
Stones and pebbles melt and
Fuse to granite fingers intruding into fractured schist.

Worse will follow. Fading, at end, the sun
Consumes the Earth,
Then blasts our atoms deep
Into lonely, lonely space.

Yet, mortal fool I be,
I place a pebble on a stone
For you, my father,
Or, maybe, me.

# Debra Wagner

## The Quaking Aspen

A bitter, cranky Crabapple tree,
and a sassy Sassafras,
gang up with a wicked Witch Hazel,
to bully a tree ~ en masse.

The petrified Quaking Aspen cries out,
*I can't stand living one moment more*
*in this cruel, unneighborly timberhood!*
So, it tugs out deep roots; lumbers down to the shore.

The wide, rushing river brims danger. It roars!
Spits out warnings the desperate Aspen ignores.
The brave tree dives in. It floats! Buoyed to the core
with past tales of calm woods ~ on the opposite shore.

Menacing clouds fling down torrents of rain;
swelling swift, swirling waters below.
Jutting boulders conspire to quell the desire
of the floater with hope for fresh life without woe.

A waterlogged Aspen was seen on a shore,
being helped by kind trees, near a wide, rushing river.
The strangest thing was ~ its leap-of-faith plunge
washed away… *every* quake; *every* quiver.

## Again

Who knew a simple game—when as a child, could make me cry—
would morph into a lifelong passion; sweet addiction; mental high?

Two baker's dozen letters churning, bubbling through my head,
wildly spew out random, valid words—from A to Zed.

My board, adorned with well-worn squares, is soundly tucked away;
yet, every day, I hear its muffled plea;

*Come play; your sister craves a win, today!*
So, we play…

My sibling's wise to my quick tricks;
yet, now, is being lured

to travel down a wayward path;
it gives me *Triple Word.*

Tiptoeing tiles on my rack
dance swiftly; shifting forth and back.

An empty pouch; the endgame nears;
and then… the **P E R F E C T** word appears!

Its seven letters calm my fear.
I place the word. We're done.

I scan her face. *Is that a tear?*
It's clear; *this* game, *I* won.

My sister's sigh absorbs the pain.
We laugh out loud…

Then play, *again*...

Then play, *again*...

Then play, *again*...

# Marsha Whitman

## Love Song

She makes the morning coffee at 10 p.m.,
leaves one light on over the sink.

He lays his clothes out the night before
gets up earlier than her in the dark,
quietly moves around, careful about the light.

She comes down when the sun is bright,
gathers her journal and devotional books,
drinks the coffee he has brought her.

From den to kitchen they email:
links to articles from the New York Times,
poems from the Writers Almanac,
recipes.

They take long walks, eat lunch and dinner together,
separate only for their long lists of things-to-do.

On the porch as the sun is setting,
They chat about how quickly the seasons transition,
aware that they finish each other's sentences,
that one for the other can always find a missing word.

## Signals

Noon of a cloudless mountain day;
lunch on the deck by the silver wind chimes.
Across the clove, magnificent Autumn on view,
smudges of burnt sienna, vermillion, ochre.
my favorites from the crayon box.

A sigh of air moves the bells together
they ring like a Tibetan call to prayer,
or our anniversary clock singing the hours.

Needing just that little encouragement to let go,
a shimmer of yellow maple leaves float to the ground,
joining the tangle of aging ferns and wildflowers below.
A spider tucks her egg sack into the window corner,
one cricket rattles intermittently.

Someone down the road has a wood fire.
I settle my sweater more closely around me,
and put another summer in my pocket.

## Christopher Seep

### **Cheap Ass Charlie** (Love on the Free Range)

Charlie was a wild mustang,
thin as a wheat stalk,
chaw-brown teeth,
skin the leather of his ancient boots,
bought when farmin' was good,
before they up and legalized it.
Proudly flexin' his mullet,
now streaked with grey,
and a dull-razor beard.
Most nights found him
at Dottie's Corrral,
a place of frugal lightin'
and cigarette smog,
with a Daisy Duke waitress
who would slap your face
if you didn't mind your manners.
Charlie sportin' his Walmart stetson,
nursin' his beer into the next millennium.
Cheap Ass.
Thought he was God's Gift,
trollin' most nights,
tryin' to entice a woman
to his single-wide.
Seems he could only get
bony-assed chicks
in sequined jeans,
with clickin' dentures
and blue prison tats,
perfumed by cigarettes and sage,

lipstick red as fresh blood,
poofed hair, lookin' all the world
like Tammy Wynette on meth.
But not so bad for
the price of a couple Schlitz.
At the trailer, the coupled
like a pair of alley dogs.
Next mornin' she wants to cuddle
like he's her Old Man,
but all Charlie's thinkin' is
about changin' the oil in the pickup
before it's too damn hot.

## Marsha Temlock

### Airplane

we travel solo
I in seat A
you in cloud B
my belt secured
you float on dreams
and feint the stars
with your wings
gravity my anchor
heaven your trapeze
to soar
to heaven
to close the space
while swallows peck my eyes.

## Janet Krauss

### Silence

"...make a poem that does not disturb the silence from which it came." —Wendell Berry

Silence creates a wide berth

for a poem to be born

and for a poem to leave

a silence behind

ringing with meaning

and a choir of images,

a silence housed

in a temple or a church,

a silence bedded

in still waters

or reflected

in a child's eyes

the first time she gazes

at the wavering flare

of a lit candle.

## An Ode to Mourning Doves

Keep on breeding—
outwitting the hunters,
keep on bringing solace to me
when I see you perched
on the porch railing making sure
to sit close to rest on each other's shoulder,
look-alikes in muted shades of grey and brown.
You take turns to warm your brood,
feed and care for your young. Seeing this,
I breathe deeply knowing all's right
with your world as long as it can be.
When you are near, I want
to hold you, wings shut tight,
shawls around your plump bodies.
Your "coo coo coo" is not a lament
but a call of endearment
that encircles my shoulders.

## Alicia Gignoux

### Bag of Almonds

Almonds huddle together in a Blue
Diamond Bag,
Whole, Natural, each one created by
One full gallon of water.
Almond tree, your blossoms bring the beekeeper
Traipsing from one orchard to another
Dropping heavy boxes on dirt, opening doors,
Begging Bees to bump each pollen laden anther
And stigma, flower to flower.
Almonds,
A pile sits on our desk and we eat.
You don't speak or spike
Sugars in my blood.
"Remove toxins; boil your almonds,"
A Rumi scholar once told me.
I wonder how his pure heart can do so?
We have a climate that boils like water and
Some have never tasted an almond, but
In bees we trust and
I crunch on the tender seed under brown skin,
Born in a velvet covered bed,
From spring blossoms
Danced on by bees,
dried by summer sun
And shucked free in the fall.

## Pamela Klem

### Epiphyte Lessons

The first orchid I ever met
was a gift presented to my grandmother
by an elegant neighbor who came for dinner.

My grandmother received it reverently
transferred the arching stems into a cobalt porcelain planter
adjusted the spires on their supporting stakes
and laid it upon the carved chest in the foyer.
So I knew it was precious, and rare.

My grandmother could make anything grow
in her long clipped contoured beds
but indoors was different.
Despite her daily mist and weak tea
and anxious hovering
that orchid was dead within months.

Great trees fall. My grandmother died
just as the daughter I named for her was born.
Some years later I took that daughter to Monteverde
where orchids attach themselves haphazardly
to decomposing logs, in jointed nooks between canopy tree branches,
the mossy bases of trees

Orchids don't rely on soil for their sustenance.
They can pull what they need from moist air and refuse
suspended particles of fog, tiny stagnant pools, half rotted
leaves

Listening to Women Talking I recoiled
when Scarface spat, *Want Less.*

There surely is a difference
between enforced wanting less
and possessing the ability to draw real sustenance
from air
and dirty wat

## Cinquains of the Day

My days
measure by sound
as reliably as
by light, as Helios crosses
my sky.

Before
I awaken
the woodpecker begins
drilling for his breakfast insects
next door.

At noon
bells toll from the
Congregational church
down the hill, reminding me to
eat lunch.

By dusk
the wafting trills
of Rachel's piano
forestalling arthritis with Chopin's
Nocturnes.

# Ed Ahern

## Fast Water Blues

Some decades ago, on the Exploits River in Newfoundland
I was fly fishing for Atlantic salmon, my guide a local
who'd befriended me, telling of his FM fishing show and
letting me meet the tolerant woman who lived with him.
He was a man of enthusiasms, vulnerably open and uncritical,
subject to the stabbings that such openness allows to happen.
And because I never judged him, he shared of himself.

Our fishing together came during paper mill visits,
wedged into evenings or a Saturday I stole from
my family so I could inject my fishing addiction.
One Saturday morning, he showed me his favorite perch,
facing the mill cross-river, and attainable only after
the mill dam's sluices were shut and the water level low.
Those nearby fished from shore, waders and staff unneeded.

The wade out was chancy, slippery rocks and brawly water,
but the salmon channeled just below, and the fishing was sweet.
That morning, I didn't hear the warning horn or it wasn't blown.
The water surged in seconds, rising from my ankles to my waist.
I was braced on my wading staff, unable to move without washing
away into a standing flume five meters tall that would carry me
over the Grand Falls. I was in a numb moment before drowning.

But he'd seen me, and grabbing a downed sapling trunk,
ran down to shore, waded in as far as he could, and
dropped the skinny trunk just upstream of me.
I wasn't rational enough to drop my tackle and grab
the bole two fisted, but did grab with my off hand,
and held on long enough for the current to swing me to shore.
When the river lowered, I went back out to his spot to fish.

I bought him dinner and left that next morning.
We never spoke unless I was on the island,
and I couldn't return for almost a year.
When I called the recording said phone disconnected.
The mill manager said the man had committed suicide,
but didn't know the specifics of where and how,
only remembering my friend as a little peculiar.

His girlfriend had left, his FM show was off air.
The obituary was vague, the relatives distant.
All I knew was that he was a gifted fisherman
who had let me fish the pool of his being
deeply enough to admire his genuineness
but not so deep as to see the roiling water
that rose to take him in a standing flume.

## Midsummer Moment

There's an unmeasured apogee in summer,
when a day holds without time or purpose,
when the sun's insistence is given its due,
when the curved apex of living hovers
listless and redolent of the sensuous,
and for that poised, weightless moment
the absence of context exudes meaning.

## About The Bards

**Sadiqua Asad**: There are two things that I ***try*** in life and enjoy trying. One of them is of course poe***try*** which the Wilton poetry group has given me a fertile soil for. The other is Chemis***try*** which I teach at Wilton High School. I always find joy in seeking the chemistry of words in poetry and the poetry of natural laws that govern chemistry.

**Edward Kabak** is a semi-retired lawyer, poet, parodist, and purported polymath. His poetry has been published before under the pseudonym Edward Kahn in the *New York Times* op-ed page titled "The House that George Built." He's also performed at public forums including presenting humorous reviews of legal events each year at a major national marketing and law conference. Among other performances, he has crafted and performed praise poems at private parties. His first book, *Provocations, Parodies, and Poetry in the Moment* will be published in early 2026. Kabak is a graduate of Columbia College and a cum laude graduate of Columbia Law School.

**D. C. Wilkinson** is a novelist, a poet, and a lifelong voyager of inner and outer realms. His literary work centers on his passion for historical tales, portal fantasies, and dreams and visions. He began his career in the Midwest as a student of Language Arts before relocating to the East Coast in his early twenties. A graduate of Columbia University and former New York City public school teacher, he now calls Connecticut his home, where he resides with his spouse and their beloved beagle.

**Wayne Lysobey** started writing short stories around 2010 and turned more towards poetry a few years after that.

Interests include rowing, fishing, skiing, chess, cooking and (of course) writing.

**Dearta Logu Fusaro's** earliest memory is the stain of a typewriter ribbon—ink bleeding red into black across her six-year-old fingers. Though the subject of that first assisted poem is lost to time, she kept the pride of it for herself. Decades later, she remains a lifelong amateur in the truest sense: one forever enamored with the music of verse. Today, she finds a creative home among the patient members of the Connecticut Poetry Society, who continue to nurture her craft. And recently published her first book title, *The Illyrian Way*, a travel memoir describing her long-distance hike along the western Balkans.

**Adele Evershed** is a Welsh writer who swapped the Valleys for the American East Coast. Her work has appeared in *Poetry Wales*, *Comstock Review*, *Modern Haiku*, *Avalon Literary Review*, *Black Bough Poetry* and *Flashflood.* She is the author of *Turbulence in Small Spaces* (Finishing Line Press) and has a forthcoming poetry collection, *In the Belly of the Wail*, with Querencia Press. She has published three novellas-in-flash—*Wannabe* and *Schooled* (Alien Buddha Press), and *A History of Hand Thrown Walls* (Unsolicited Press). Her short story collection, *Suffer/Rage*, was released by Dark Myth Publications.

**Francie Grace** has been a writer since birth and remembers as a young girl viewing as rivals the authors depicted in a literary deck of cards. Francie is best known as a journalist who had a very long run at CBS News. She has many creative pursuits including poetry, screenwriting, songwriting, and art (franciegraceart.com).

**Ray Rauth:** for years he searched for his poetic voice. He never found it. But as the decade-long leader of the Wilton Poetry Workshop, he helped scads of others find theirs.

**Debra Wagner** is a fledgling poet, who recently leapt from the comfort and privacy of the nest, to feel the thrill of the winds beneath her newfound wings.

**Marsha Whitman's** career has been spent in music as teacher, choral conductor, arranger, impresario, singer and accompanist. She has always kept journals of everyday experiences and poetry. *Holding the Body Back* (1st World Publishing, 2020) is her one full length book of poetry. Her work has been published in the anthology *Pandemic Puzzle Poems* (Blue Light Press). Born (1951) and raised in Norwalk, CT, USA.

**Christopher Seep** scatters words on a fallow page, hoping to grow a poem.

**Marsha Temlock** is the author of *Your Child's Divorce: What to Expect... What You Can Do*, *The Exile*, a young adult novel, and *Tuesday's Mah Jongg is More Than a Game, a novel.* She has appeared on the Today Show and was featured in the *New York Times*, *The Wall Street Journal*, the *Miami Herald*, and interviewed on dozens of radio talk shows. She holds a master of arts in English from NYU and a master of arts in organizational psychology from Columbia University. She taught literature and writing at Fairfield University, Sacred Heart University, and Norwalk Community College. Her interests include theater, literature, travel, and (of course) Mah Jongg. Learn more at tuesdaymahjongg.com.

**Janet Krauss** retired after thirty-nine years of teaching English at Fairfield University. She continues to mentor students, lead a poetry discussion at the Wilton Library, and participate in the CT Poetry Society Workshop and other poetry groups. She co-leads the Poetry Program of the Black Rock Art Guild. She has two books of poetry: *Borrowed Scenery (*Yuganta Press) and *Through the Trees of Autumn* (*Spartina* Press). Many of her poems have been published in *Amethyst Literary Journal* and her haikus in *Cold Moon Journal.*

**Alicia Gignoux** spends time in Wilton from time to time. She has enjoyed sharing poems and listening to the poems that the Connecticut folks bring to the library.

**Pam Klem** lives in Wilton, CT with her husband Tom and her dog Lester. She is a longtime reader of poetry, and recently returned to writing it after a decades-long hiatus. Her poems have appeared in *Thimble Literary Magazine* and an upcoming anthology by Orenaug Mountain Publishers.

**Ed Ahern** resumed writing after forty-odd years in foreign intelligence and international sales. He's had over 600 stories and poems published so far, and twelve books. He works the other side of writing at *Bewildering Stories,* where he squats on the review board, and at *ScribesMICRO*, where he's the idle figurehead.

## Blurb:

The Wilton, CT Poetry Group keeps it personal. The hollow square tables place everyone live and face to face, Members present their best work for constructive critiquing, and the poems you'll read here were tempered by this process. Some lighthearted, some melancholy, all meant to be approachable. We hope you'll enjoy reading them as much as we did creating them.

www.ingramcontent.com/pod-product-compliance
Lightning Source LLC
LaVergne TN
LVHW050947080826
845145LV00004B/1446

*9781949122268*